APHRODITE

APEX

By Christine Ha

WWW.APEXEDITIONS.COM

Apex is distributed by North Star Editions:
sales@northstareditions.com | 888-417-0195

Produced for Apex by Red Line Editorial.

Photographs ©: Shutterstock Images, cover, 1, 4–5, 6–7, 8–9, 10–11, 12, 12–13, 14–15, 16–17, 19, 20–21, 22–23, 25, 26–27, 29; History and Art Collection/Alamy, 18; iStockphoto, 24

Library of Congress Control Number: 2020952913

ISBN
978-1-63738-010-9 (hardcover)
978-1-63738-046-8 (paperback)
978-1-63738-116-8 (ebook pdf)
978-1-63738-082-6 (hosted ebook)

Printed in the United States of America
Mankato, MN
082021

NOTE TO PARENTS AND EDUCATORS

Apex books are designed to build literacy skills in striving readers. Exciting, high-interest content attracts and holds readers' attention. The text is carefully leveled to allow students to achieve success quickly. Additional features, such as bolded glossary words for difficult terms, help build comprehension.

TABLE OF CONTENTS

CHAPTER 1

FATEFUL RACE

Hippomenes was sad. He loved Atalanta. But she would only marry whoever could beat her in a race. And she was very fast.

A statue in France shows Atalanta racing.

Hippomenes used Aphrodite's golden apples in a race against Atalanta.

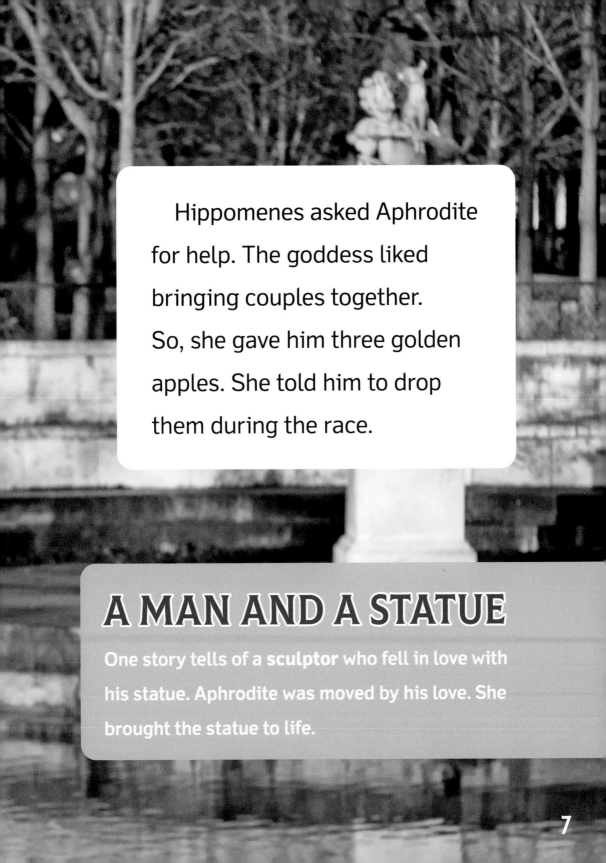

Hippomenes asked Aphrodite for help. The goddess liked bringing couples together. So, she gave him three golden apples. She told him to drop them during the race.

A MAN AND A STATUE

One story tells of a **sculptor** who fell in love with his statue. Aphrodite was moved by his love. She brought the statue to life.

The goddess Aphrodite had great power.

At first, Atalanta took the lead. But she stopped to pick up the apples. She fell behind, and Hippomenes won. Now he could marry his love.

In Greek myths, golden apples were often gifts or prizes. But sometimes they caused fights.

CHAPTER 2

GODDESS OF LOVE

Aphrodite was the Greek goddess of love. She was the goddess of beauty, too. She was very pretty.

The Romans had their own versions of Greek gods. The Roman goddess of love was called Venus.

Legends say she was born near the island of Cyprus. But she was never a baby. Instead, she rose up out of the ocean. Then she floated to shore.

Ruins of a temple for Aphrodite still stand in Cyprus.

According to legend, Aphrodite came from the ocean near Cyprus.

Some people said Aphrodite protected sailors.

In one legend, Aphrodite's tears created red flowers when a person she loved died.

Aphrodite could make people fall in and out of love. She fell in love, too. She loved both gods and humans.

A MAGIC BELT

Aphrodite wore a **girdle**. It had magical powers. Humans and gods would fall in love with whoever was wearing it.

Aphrodite married Hephaestus. He was the god of fire and metalworking.

CHAPTER 3

MOST BEAUTIFUL

Once, three goddesses fought over who was most beautiful. A man named Paris was asked to decide. But each goddess tried to **bribe** him.

Paris and Helen were two people that Aphrodite brought together.

Athena (left) and Hera (right) were two of the main Greek goddesses.

Athena promised to help Paris win wars. Hera offered to make him a ruler. Aphrodite said the most beautiful woman in the world would be his wife.

The woman's name was Helen. Her husband was the king of Sparta.

Aphrodite sometimes punished people. She made Narcissus fall in love with his reflection.

Eros is better known by his Roman name, Cupid. He is often shown with wings.

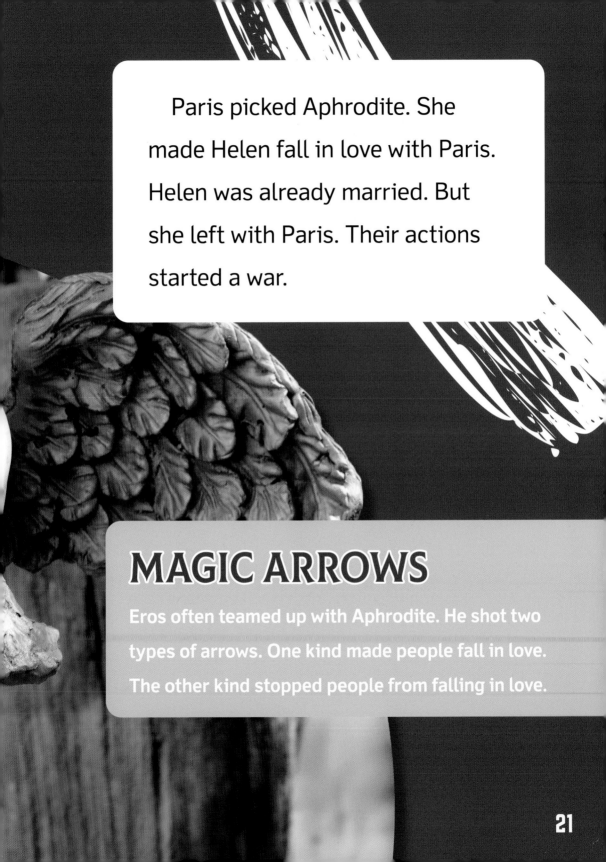

Paris picked Aphrodite. She made Helen fall in love with Paris. Helen was already married. But she left with Paris. Their actions started a war.

MAGIC ARROWS

Eros often teamed up with Aphrodite. He shot two types of arrows. One kind made people fall in love. The other kind stopped people from falling in love.

CHAPTER 4

HONORING APHRODITE

Aphrodite was a **popular** goddess. People prayed to her for help with love and marriage. She could even change how people looked.

In some cities, people honored Aphrodite as a war goddess.

Aphrodite's main places of **worship** were in Cyprus. But she had followers all over Greece. She also had temples in the surrounding areas.

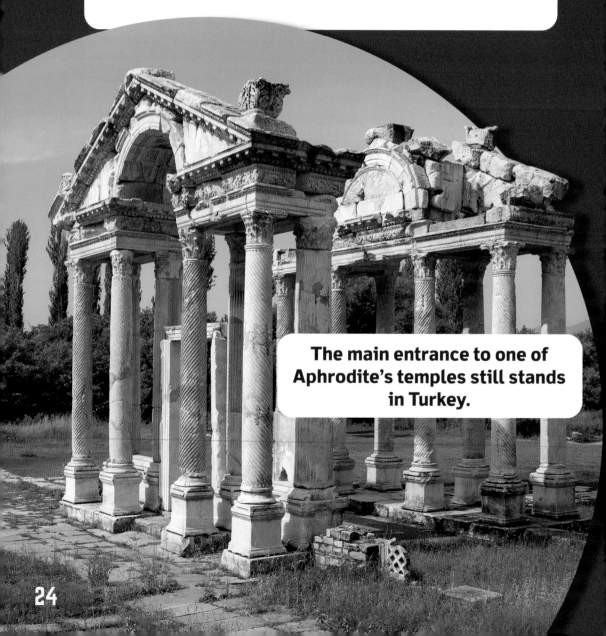

The main entrance to one of Aphrodite's temples still stands in Turkey.

Several cities were dedicated to the goddess Aphrodite.

A BIG FESTIVAL

The people of Cyprus held a **festival** each year. It honored Aphrodite. The festival took place in spring. It lasted several days.

Shells and mirrors were important to Aphrodite. So were swans. People brought these things to her temples. They also offered **incense** and flowers.

Stories of Aphrodite have inspired many famous works of art.

In some stories, Aphrodite rode a golden chariot. A team of doves pulled it.

COMPREHENSION QUESTIONS

Write your answers on a separate piece of paper.

1. Write a few sentences explaining the main ideas of Chapter 4.

2. Do you think it would be more helpful to make people fall in love or out of love? Why?

3. Which goddess did Paris choose as the most beautiful?

    A. Aphrodite

    B. Athena

    C. Hera

4. Why might shells be a symbol of Aphrodite?

    A. Shells come from the ocean, where she was born.

    B. Shells come from animals, which she ruled.

    C. Shells can hold pearls, which she wore.

5. What does **followers** mean in this book?

*Aphrodite's main places of worship were in Cyprus. But she had **followers** all over Greece.*

    A. people who get lost

    B. people who believe in a god or goddess

    C. people who cook food

6. What does **offered** mean in this book?

*People brought these things to her temples. They also **offered** incense and flowers.*

    A. gave something to a goddess

    B. sold something at a store

    C. lost something at sea

Answer key on page 32.

GLOSSARY

bribe
To give someone gifts or money to sway a choice or action.

chariot
A two-wheeled cart pulled by horses or other animals.

festival
A day or time of celebration, often based on a religion.

girdle
A belt or cord that is worn around the waist.

incense
A spice that is burned to make a sweet smell.

myths
Well-known stories from the past that often include magic.

popular
Liked by or known to many people.

protected
Watched over or kept safe.

sculptor
A person who carves art from stone, wood, or other hard materials.

worship
The ways people honor or pray to a god or goddess.

TO LEARN MORE

BOOKS

Bell, Samantha S. *Ancient Greece.* Lake Elmo, MN: Focus Readers, 2020.

Buckey, A. W. *Greek Gods, Heroes, and Mythology.* Minneapolis: Abdo Publishing, 2019.

Temple, Teri. *Aphrodite: Goddess of Love and Beauty.* Mankato, MN: The Child's World, 2019.

ONLINE RESOURCES

Visit **www.apexeditions.com** to find links and resources related to this title.

ABOUT THE AUTHOR

Christine Ha lives in Minnesota. She enjoys reading and learning about myths and legends from around the world.

INDEX

Answer Key:
1. Answers will vary; **2.** Answers will vary; **3.** A; **4.** A; **5.** B; **6.** A